D1137230

WINTER TREES

by the same author

THE BELL JAR
JOHNNY PANIC AND THE BIBLE OF DREAMS
★
THE COLOSSUS
ARIEL
CROSSING THE WATER
COLLECTED POEMS
SELECTED POEMS
★
THE BED BOOK
★
LETTERS HOME:
CORRESPONDENCE 1950–65

SYLVIA PLATH

Winter Trees

faber and faber
LONDON · BOSTON

First published in 1971
by Faber and Faber Limited
3 Queen Square London WC1N 3AU
Reprinted 1972
First published in this edition 1975
Reprinted 1976, 1978, 1982 and 1987

Printed in Great Britain by
Redwood Burn Limited, Trowbridge, Wiltshire and
bound by Pegasus Bookbinding, Melksham, Wiltshire
All rights reserved

ISBN 0 571 10862 8 (Faber Paperbacks)
ISBN 0 571 09739 1 (hard-bound edition)

NOTE

The poems in this volume are all out of the batch from which the *Ariel* poems were more or less arbitrarily chosen and they were all composed in the last nine months of Sylvia Plath's life.

'Three Women', A Poem for Three Voices, was written slightly earlier and can be seen as a bridge between *The Colossus* and *Ariel*, both in the change of style from the first half to the last and in that it was written to be read aloud. Sylvia Plath has said that about this time she began to compose her poems more to be read aloud and this piece may well have played a big part in this technical development.

T. H.

CONTENTS

WINTER TREES

The wet dawn inks are doing their blue dissolve.
On their blotter of fog the trees
Seem a botanical drawing—
Memories growing, ring on ring,
A series of weddings.

Knowing neither abortions nor bitchery,
Truer than women,
They seed so effortlessly!
Tasting the winds, that are footless,
Waist-deep in history—

Full of wings, otherworldliness.
In this, they are Ledas.
O mother of leaves and sweetness
Who are these pietas?
The shadows of ringdoves chanting, but easing nothing.

CHILD

Your clear eye is the one absolutely beautiful thing.
I want to fill it with colour and ducks,
The zoo of the new

Whose names you meditate—
April snowdrop, Indian pipe,
Little

Stalk without wrinkle,
Pool in which images
Should be grand and classical

Not this troublous
Wringing of hands, this dark
Ceiling without a star.

BRASILIA

Will they occur,
These people with torsos of steel
Winged elbows and eyeholes

Awaiting masses
Of cloud to give them expression,
These super-people!—

And my baby a nail
Driven, driven in.
He shrieks in his grease

Bones nosing for distances.
And I, nearly extinct,
His three teeth cutting

Themselves on my thumb—
And the star,
The old story.

In the lane I meet sheep and wagons,
Red earth, motherly blood.
O You who eat

People like light rays, leave
This one
Mirror safe, unredeemed

By the dove's annihilation,
The glory
The power, the glory.

GIGOLO

Pocket watch, I tick well.
The streets are lizardy crevices
Sheer-sided, with holes where to hide.
It is best to meet in a cul-de-sac,

A palace of velvet
With windows of mirrors.
There one is safe,
There are no family photographs,

No rings through the nose, no cries
Bright fish hooks, the smiles of women
Gulp at my bulk
And I, in my snazzy blacks,

Mill a litter of breasts like jellyfish.
To nourish
The cellos of moans I eat eggs—
Eggs and fish, the essentials,

The aphrodisiac squid.
My mouth sags,
The mouth of Christ
When my engine reaches the end of it.

The tattle of my
Gold joints, my way of turning
Bitches to ripples of silver
Rolls out a carpet, a hush.

And there is no end, no end of it.
I shall never grow old. New oysters
Shriek in the sea and I
Glitter like Fontainebleau

Gratified,
All the fall of water an eye
Over whose pool I tenderly
Lean and see me.

CHILDLESS WOMAN

The womb
Rattles its pod, the moon
Discharges itself from the tree with nowhere to go.

My landscape is a hand with no lines,
The roads bunched to a knot,
The knot myself,

Myself the rose you achieve—
This body,
This ivory

Godly as a child's shriek.
Spiderlike, I spin mirrors,
Loyal to my image,

Uttering nothing but blood—
Taste it, dark red!
And my forest

My funeral,
And this hill and this
Gleaming with the mouths of corpses.

PURDAH

Jade—
Stone of the side,
The agonized

Side of green Adam, I
Smile, cross-legged,
Enigmatical,

Shifting my clarities.
So valuable!
How the sun polishes this shoulder!

And should
The moon, my
Indefatigable cousin

Rise, with her cancerous pallors,
Dragging trees—
Little bushy polyps,

Little nets,
My visibilities hide.
I gleam like a mirror.

At this facet the bridegroom arrives
Lord of the mirrors!
It is himself he guides

In among these silk
Screens, these rustling appurtenances.
I breathe, and the mouth

Veil stirs its curtain
My eye
Veil is

A concatenation of rainbows.
I am his.
Even in his

Absence, I
Revolve in my
Sheath of impossibles,

Priceless and quiet
Among these parakeets, macaws!
O chatterers

Attendants of the eyelash!
I shall unloose
On feather, like the peacock.

Attendants of the lip!
I shall unloose
One note

Shattering
The chandelier
Of air that all day flies

Its crystals
A million ignorants.
Attendants!

Attendants!
And at his next step
I shall unloose

I shall unloose—
From the small jewelled
Doll he guards like a heart—

The lioness,
The shriek in the bath,
The cloak of holes.

THE COURAGE OF SHUTTING-UP

The courage of the shut mouth, in spite of artillery!
The line pink and quiet, a worm, basking.
There are black discs behind it, the discs of outrage,
And the outrage of a sky, the lined brain of it.
The discs revolve, they ask to be heard—

Loaded, as they are, with accounts of bastardies.
Bastardies, usages, desertions and doubleness,
The needle journeying in its groove,
Silver beast between two dark canyons,
A great surgeon, now a tattooist,

Tattooing over and over the same blue grievances,
The snakes, the babies, the tits
On mermaids and two-legged dreamgirls.
The surgeon is quiet, he does not speak.
He has seen too much death, his hands are full of it.

So the discs of the brain revolve, like the muzzles of cannon.
Then there is that antique billhook, the tongue,
Indefatigable, purple. Must it be cut out?
It has nine tails, it is dangerous.
And the noise it flays from the air, once it gets going!

No, the tongue, too, has been put by,
Hung up in the library with the engravings of Rangoon
And the fox heads, the otter heads, the heads of dead rabbits.
It is a marvellous object—
The things it has pierced in its time.

But how about the eyes, the eyes, the eyes?
Mirrors can kill and talk, they are terrible rooms
In which a torture goes on one can only watch.
The face that lived in this mirror is the face of a dead man.
Do not worry about the eyes—

They may be white and shy, they are no stool pigeons,
Their death rays folded like flags
Of a country no longer heard of,
An obstinate independency
Insolvent among the mountains.

THE OTHER

You come in late, wiping your lips.
What did I leave untouched on the doorstep—

White Nike,
Streaming between my walls?

Smilingly, blue lightning
Assumes, like a meathook, the burden of his parts.

The police love you, you confess everything.
Bright hair, shoe-black, old plastic,

Is my life so intriguing?
Is it for this you widen your eye-rings?

Is it for this the air motes depart?
They are not air motes, they are corpuscles.

Open your handbag. What is that bad smell?
It is your knitting, busily

Hooking itself to itself,
It is your sticky candies.

I have your head on my wall.
Navel cords, blue-red and lucent,

Shriek from my belly like arrows, and these I ride.
O moon-glow, o sick one,

The stolen horses, the fornications
Circle a womb of marble.

Where are you going
That you suck breath like mileage?

Sulphurous adulteries grieve in a dream.
Cold glass, how you insert yourself

Between myself and myself.
I scratch like a cat.

The blood that runs is dark fruit—
An effect, a cosmetic.

You smile.
No, it is not fatal.

STOPPED DEAD

A squeal of brakes.
Or is it a birth cry?
And here we are, hung out over the dead drop
Uncle, pants factory Fatso, millionaire.
And you out cold beside me in your chair.

The wheels, two rubber grubs, bite their sweet tails.
Is that Spain down there?
Red and yellow, two passionate hot metals
Writhing and sighing, what sort of a scenery is it?
It isn't England, it isn't France, it isn't Ireland.

It's violent. We're here on a visit,
With a goddam baby screaming off somewhere.
There's always a bloody baby in the air.
I'd call it a sunset, but
Whoever heard a sunset yowl like that?

You are sunk in your seven chins, still as a ham.
Who do you think I am,
Uncle, uncle?
Sad Hamlet, with a knife?
Where do you stash your life?

Is it a penny, a pearl—
Your soul, your soul?
I'll carry it off like a rich pretty girl,
Simply open the door and step out of the car
And live in Gibraltar on air, on air.

THE RABBIT CATCHER

It was a place of force—
The wind gagging my mouth with my own blown hair,
Tearing off my voice, and the sea
Blinding me with its lights, the lives of the dead
Unreeling in it, spreading like oil.

I tasted the malignity of the gorse,
Its black spikes,
The extreme unction of its yellow candle-flowers.
They had an efficiency, a great beauty,
And were extravagant, like torture.

There was only one place to get to.
Simmering, perfumed,
The paths narrowed into the hollow.
And the snares almost effaced themselves—
Zeroes, shutting on nothing,

Set close, like birth pangs.
The absence of shrieks
Made a hole in the hot day, a vacancy.
The glassy light was a clear wall,
The thickets quiet.

I felt a still busyness, an intent.
I felt hands round a tea mug, dull, blunt,
Ringing the white china.
How they awaited him, those little deaths!
They waited like sweethearts. They excited him.

And we, too, had a relationship—
Tight wires between us,
Pegs too deep to uproot, and a mind like a ring
Sliding shut on some quick thing,
The constriction killing me also.

MYSTIC

The air is a mill of hooks—
Questions without answer,
Glittering and drunk as flies
Whose kiss stings unbearably
In the fetid wombs of black air under pines in summer.

I remember
The dead smell of sun on wood cabins,
The stiffness of sails, the long salt winding sheets.
Once one has seen God, what is the remedy?
Once one has been seized up

Without a part left over,
Not a toe, not a finger, and used,
Used utterly, in the sun's conflagrations, the stains
That lengthen from ancient cathedrals
What is the remedy?

The pill of the Communion tablet,
The walking beside still water? Memory?
Or picking up the bright pieces
Of Christ in the faces of rodents,
The tame flower-nibblers, the ones

Whose hopes are so low they are comfortable—
The humpback in her small, washed cottage
Under the spokes of the clematis.
Is there no great love, only tenderness?
Does the sea

Remember the walker upon it?
Meaning leaks from the molecules.

The chimneys of the city breathe, the window sweats,
The children leap in their cots.
The sun blooms, it is a geranium.

The heart has not stopped.

BY CANDLELIGHT

This is winter, this is night, small love—
A sort of black horsehair,
A rough, dumb country stuff
Steeled with the sheen
Of what green stars can make it to our gate.
I hold you on my arm.
It is very late.
The dull bells tongue the hour.
The mirror floats us at one candle power.

This is the fluid in which we meet each other,
This haloey radiance that seems to breathe
And lets our shadows wither
Only to blow
Them huge again, violent giants on the wall.
One match scratch makes you real.
At first the candle will not bloom at all—
It snuffs its bud
To almost nothing, to a dull blue dud.

I hold my breath until you creak to life,
Balled hedgehog,
Small and cross. The yellow knife
Grows tall. You clutch your bars.
My singing makes you roar.
I rock you like a boat
Across the Indian carpet, the cold floor,
While the brass man
Kneels, back bent, as best he can

Hefting his white pillar with the light
That keeps the sky at bay,
The sack of black! It is everywhere, tight, tight!

He is yours, the little brassy Atlas—
Poor heirloom, all you have,
At his heels a pile of five brass cannonballs,
No child, no wife.
Five balls! Five bright brass balls!
To juggle with, my love, when the sky falls.

LYONNESSE

No use whistling for Lyonnesse!
Sea-cold, sea-cold it certainly is.
Take a look at the white, high berg on his forehead—

There's where it sunk.
The blue, green,
Grey, indeterminate gilt

Sea of his eyes washing over it
And a round bubble
Popping upward from the mouths of bells

People and cows.
The Lyonians had always thought
Heaven would be something else,

But with the same faces,
The same places . . .
It was not a shock—

The clear, green, quite breathable atmosphere,
Cold grits underfoot,
And the spidery water-dazzle on field and street.

It never occurred that they had been forgot,
That the big God
Had lazily closed one eye and let them slip

Over the English cliff and under so much history!
They did not see him smile,
Turn, like an animal,

In his cage of ether, his cage of stars.
He'd had so many wars!
The white gape of his mind was the real Tabula Rasa.

THALIDOMIDE

O half moon—

Half-brain, luminosity—
Negro, masked like a white,

Your dark
Amputations crawl and appal—

Spidery, unsafe.
What glove

What leatheriness
Has protected

Me from that shadow—
The indelible buds,

Knuckles at shoulder-blades, the
Faces that

Shove into being, dragging
The lopped

Blood-caul of absences.
All night I carpenter

A space for the thing I am given,
A love

Of two wet eyes and a screech.
White spit

Of indifference!
The dark fruits revolve and fall.

The glass cracks across,
The image

Flees and aborts like dropped mercury.

FOR A FATHERLESS SON

You will be aware of an absence, presently,
Growing beside you, like a tree,
A death tree, colour gone, an Australian gum tree—
Balding, gelded by lightning—an illusion,
And a sky like a pig's backside, an utter lack of attention.

But right now you are dumb.
And I love your stupidity,
The blind mirror of it. I look in
And find no face but my own, and you think that's funny.
It is good for me

To have you grab my nose, a ladder rung.
One day you may touch what's wrong
The small skulls, the smashed blue hills, the godawful hush.
Till then your smiles are found money.

LESBOS

Viciousness in the kitchen!
The potatoes hiss.
It is all Hollywood, windowless,
The fluorescent light wincing on and off like a terrible
    migraine,
Coy paper strips for doors—
Stage curtains, a widow's frizz.
And I, love, am a pathological liar,
And my child—look at her, face down on the floor,
Little unstrung puppet, kicking to disappear—
Why she is schizophrenic,
Her face red and white, a panic,
You have stuck her kittens outside your window
In a sort of cement well
Where they crap and puke and cry and she can't hear.
You say you can't stand her,
The bastard's a girl.
You who have blown your tubes like a bad radio
Clear of voices and history, the staticky
Noise of the new.
You say I should drown the kittens. Their smell!
You say I should drown my girl.
She'll cut her throat at ten if she's mad at two.
The baby smiles, fat snail,
From the polished lozenges of orange linoleum.
You could eat him. He's a boy.
You say your husband is just no good to you.
His Jew-Mama guards his sweet sex like a pearl.
You have one baby, I have two.
I should sit on a rock off Cornwall and comb my hair.
I should wear tiger pants, I should have an affair.
We should meet in another life, we should meet in air,
Me and you.

Meanwhile there's a stink of fat and baby crap.
I'm doped and thick from my last sleeping pill.
The smog of cooking, the smog of hell
Floats our heads, two venomous opposites,
Our bones, our hair.
I call you Orphan, orphan. You are ill.
The sun gives you ulcers, the wind gives you T.B.
Once you were beautiful.
In New York, in Hollywood, the men said: 'Through?
Gee baby, you are rare.'
You acted, acted, acted for the thrill.
The impotent husband slumps out for a coffee.
I try to keep him in,
An old pole for the lightning,
The acid baths, the skyfuls off of you.
He lumps it down the plastic cobbled hill,
Flogged trolley. The sparks are blue.
The blue sparks spill,
Splitting like quartz into a million bits.

O jewel! O valuable!
That night the moon
Dragged its blood bag, sick
Animal
Up over the harbour lights.
And then grew normal,
Hard and apart and white.
The scale-sheen on the sand scared me to death.
We kept picking up handfuls, loving it,
Working it like dough, a mulatto body,
The silk grits.
A dog picked up your doggy husband. He went on.

Now I am silent, hate
Up to my neck,
Thick, thick.

I do not speak.
I am packing the hard potatoes like good clothes,
I am packing the babies,
I am packing the sick cats.
O vase of acid,
It is love you are full of. You know who you hate.
He is hugging his ball and chain down by the gate
That opens to the sea
Where it drives in, white and black,
Then spews it back.
Every day you fill him with soul-stuff, like a pitcher.
You are so exhausted.
Your voice my ear-ring,
Flapping and sucking, blood-loving bat.
That is that. That is that.
You peer from the door,
Sad hag. 'Every woman's a whore.
I can't communicate.'

I see your cute décor
Close on you like the fist of a baby
Or an anemone, that sea
Sweetheart, that kleptomaniac.
I am still raw.
I say I may be back.
You know what lies are for.

Even in your Zen heaven we shan't meet.

THE SWARM

Somebody is shooting at something in our town—
A dull pom, pom in the Sunday street.
Jealousy can open the blood,
It can make black roses.
Who are they shooting at?

It is you the knives are out for
At Waterloo, Waterloo, Napoleon,
The hump of Elba on your short back,
And the snow, marshalling its brilliant cutlery
Mass after mass, saying Shh!

Shh! These are chess people you play with,
Still figures of ivory.
The mud squirms with throats,
Stepping stones for French bootsoles.
The gilt and pink domes of Russia melt and float off

In the furnace of greed. Clouds, clouds.
So the swarm balls and deserts
Seventy feet up, in a black pine tree.
It must be shot down. Pom! Pom!
So dumb it thinks bullets are thunder.

It thinks they are the voice of God
Condoning the beak, the claw, the grin of the dog
Yellow-haunched, a pack-dog,
Grinning over its bone of ivory
Like the pack, the pack, like everybody.

The bees have got so far. Seventy feet high!
Russia, Poland and Germany!
The mild hills, the same old magenta
Fields shrunk to a penny
Spun into a river, the river crossed.

The bees argue, in their black ball,
A flying hedgehog, all prickles.
The man with grey hands stands under the honeycomb
Of their dream, the hived station
Where trains, faithful to their steel arcs,

Leave and arrive, and there is no end to the country.
Pom! Pom! They fall
Dismembered, to a tod of ivy.
So much for the charioteers, the outriders, the Grand Army!
A red tatter, Napoleon!

The last badge of victory.
The swarm is knocked into a cocked straw hat.
Elba, Elba, bleb on the sea!
The white busts of marshalls, admirals, generals
Worming themselves into niches.

How instructive this is!
The dumb, banded bodies
Walking the plank draped with Mother France's upholstery
Into a new mausoleum,
An ivory palace, a crotch pine.

The man with grey hands smiles—
The smile of a man of business, intensely practical.
They are not hands at all
But asbestos receptacles.
Pom! Pom! 'They would have killed *me*'.

Stings big as drawing pins!
It seems bees have a notion of honour,
A black intractable mind.
Napoleon is pleased, he is pleased with everything.
O Europe! O ton of honey!

MARY'S SONG

The Sunday lamb cracks in its fat.
The fat
Sacrifices its opacity. . . .

A window, holy gold.
The fire makes it precious,
The same fire

Melting the tallow heretics,
Ousting the Jews.
Their thick palls float

Over the cicatrix of Poland, burnt-out
Germany.
They do not die.

Grey birds obsess my heart,
Mouth-ash, ash of eye.
They settle. On the high

Precipice
That emptied one man into space
The ovens glowed like heavens, incandescent.

It is a heart,
This holocaust I walk in,
O golden child the world will kill and eat.

THREE WOMEN

A Poem for Three Voices

Setting : A Maternity Ward and round about

FIRST VOICE:
I am slow as the world. I am very patient,
Turning through my time, the suns and stars
Regarding me with attention.
The moon's concern is more personal:
She passes and repasses, luminous as a nurse.
Is she sorry for what will happen? I do not think so.
She is simply astonished at fertility.

When I walk out, I am a great event.
I do not have to think, or even rehearse.
What happens in me will happen without attention.
The pheasant stands on the hill;
He is arranging his brown feathers.
I cannot help smiling at what it is I know.
Leaves and petals attend me. I am ready.

SECOND VOICE:
When I first saw it, the small red seep, I did not believe it.
I watched the men walk about me in the office. They were so
    flat!
There was something about them like cardboard, and now I
    had caught it,
That flat, flat, flatness from which ideas, destructions,
Bulldozers, guillotines, white chambers of shrieks proceed,
Endlessly proceed—and the cold angels, the abstractions.
I sat at my desk in my stockings, my high heels,

And the man I work for laughed: 'Have you seen something
   awful?
You are so white, suddenly.' And I said nothing.
I saw death in the bare trees, a deprivation.
I could not believe it. Is it so difficult
For the spirit to conceive a face, a mouth?
The letters proceed from these black keys, and these black
   keys proceed
From my alphabetical fingers, ordering parts,

Parts, bits, cogs, the shining multiples.
I am dying as I sit. I lose a dimension.
Trains roar in my ears, departures, departures!
The silver track of time empties into the distance,
The white sky empties of its promise, like a cup.
These are my feet, these mechanical echoes.
Tap, tap, tap, steel pegs. I am found wanting.

This is a disease I carry home, this is a death.
Again, this is a death. Is it the air,
The particles of destruction I suck up? Am I a pulse
That wanes and wanes, facing the cold angel?
Is this my lover then? This death, this death?
As a child I loved a lichen-bitten name.
Is this the one sin then, this old dead love of death?

THIRD VOICE:
I remember the minute when I knew for sure.
The willows were chilling,
The face in the pool was beautiful, but not mine—
It had a consequential look, like everything else,
And all I could see was dangers: doves and words,
Stars and showers of gold—conceptions, conceptions!
I remember a white, cold wing

And the great swan, with its terrible look,
Coming at me, like a castle, from the top of the river.
There is a snake in swans.
He glided by; his eye had a black meaning.
I saw the world in it—small, mean and black,
Every little word hooked to every little word, and act to act.
A hot blue day had budded into something.

I wasn't ready. The white clouds rearing
Aside were dragging me in four directions.
I wasn't ready.
I had no reverence.
I thought I could deny the consequence—
But it was too late for that. It was too late, and the face
Went on shaping itself with love, as if I was ready.

SECOND VOICE:
It is a world of snow now. I am not at home.
How white these sheets are. The faces have no features.
They are bald and impossible, like the faces of my children,
Those little sick ones that elude my arms.
Other children do not touch me: they are terrible.
They have too many colours, too much life. They are not
    quiet,
Quiet, like the little emptinesses I carry.

I have had my chances. I have tried and tried.
I have stitched life into me like a rare organ,
And walked carefully, precariously, like something rare.
I have tried not to think too hard. I have tried to be natural.
I have tried to be blind in love, like other women,
Blind in my bed, with my dear blind sweet one,
Not looking, through the thick dark, for the face of another.

I did not look. But still the face was there,
The face of the unborn one that loved its perfections,

The face of the dead one that could only be perfect
In its easy peace, could only keep holy so.
And then there were other faces. The faces of nations,
Governments, parliaments, societies,
The faceless faces of important men.

It is these men I mind:
They are so jealous of anything that is not flat! They are
    jealous gods
That would have the whole world flat because they are.
I see the Father conversing with the Son.
Such flatness cannot but be holy.
'Let us make a heaven,' they say.
'Let us flatten and launder the grossness from these souls.'

FIRST VOICE:
I am calm. I am calm. It is the calm before something awful:
The yellow minute before the wind walks, when the leaves
Turn up their hands, their pallors. It is so quiet here.
The sheets, the faces, are white and stopped, like clocks.
Voices stand back and flatten. Their visible hieroglyphs
Flatten to parchment screens to keep the wind off.
They paint such secrets in Arabic, Chinese!

I am dumb and brown. I am a seed about to break.
The brownness is my dead self, and it is sullen:
It does not wish to be more, or different.
Dusk hoods me in blue now, like a Mary.
O colour of distance and forgetfulness!—
When will it be, the second when Time breaks
And eternity engulfs it, and I drown utterly?

I talk to myself, myself only, set apart—
Swabbed and lurid with disinfectants, sacrificial.
Waiting lies heavy on my lids. It lies like sleep,
Like a big sea. Far off, far off, I feel the first wave tug

Its cargo of agony toward me, inescapable, tidal.
And I, a shell, echoing on this white beach
Face the voices that overwhelm, the terrible element.

THIRD VOICE:
I am a mountain now, among mountainy women.
The doctors move among us as if our bigness
Frightened the mind. They smile like fools.
They are to blame for what I am, and they know it.
They hug their flatness like a kind of health.
And what if they found themselves surprised, as I did?
They would go mad with it.

And what if two lives leaked between my thighs?
I have seen the white clean chamber with its instruments.
It is a place of shrieks. It is not happy.
'This is where you will come when you are ready.'
The night lights are flat red moons. They are dull with blood.
I am not ready for anything to happen.
I should have murdered this, that murders me.

FIRST VOICE:
There is no miracle more cruel than this.
I am dragged by the horses, the iron hooves.
I last. I last it out. I accomplish a work.
Dark tunnel, through which hurtle the visitations,
The visitations, the manifestations, the startled faces.
I am the centre of an atrocity.
What pains, what sorrows must I be mothering?

Can such innocence kill and kill? It milks my life.
The trees wither in the street. The rain is corrosive.
I taste it on my tongue, and the workable horrors,
The horrors that stand and idle, the slighted godmothers
With their hearts that tick and tick, with their satchels of
    instruments.

I shall be a wall and a roof, protecting.
I shall be a sky and a hill of good: O let me be!

A power is growing on me, an old tenacity.
I am breaking apart like the world. There is this blackness,
This ram of blackness. I fold my hands on a mountain.
The air is thick. It is thick with this working.
I am used. I am drummed into use.
My eyes are squeezed by this blackness.
I see nothing.

SECOND VOICE:
I am accused. I dream of massacres.
I am a garden of black and red agonies. I drink them,
Hating myself, hating and fearing. And now the world conceives
  ceives
Its end and runs toward it, arms held out in love.
It is a love of death that sickens everything.
A dead sun stains the newsprint. It is red.
I lose life after life. The dark earth drinks them.

She is the vampire of us all. So she supports us,
Fattens us, is kind. Her mouth is red.
I know her. I know her intimately—
Old winter-face, old barren one, old time bomb.
Men have used her meanly. She will eat them.
Eat them, eat them, eat them in the end.
The sun is down. I die. I make a death.

FIRST VOICE:
Who is he, this blue, furious boy,
Shiny and strange, as if he had hurtled from a star?
He is looking so angrily!
He flew into the room, a shriek at his heel.
The blue colour pales. He is human after all.
A red lotus opens in its bowl of blood;
They are stitching me up with silk, as if I were a material.

45

What did my fingers do before they held him?
What did my heart do, with its love?
I have never seen a thing so clear.
His lids are like the lilac-flower
And soft as a moth, his breath.
I shall not let go.
There is no guile or warp in him. May he keep so.

SECOND VOICE:
There is the moon in the high window. It is over.
How winter fills my soul! And that chalk light
Laying its scales on the windows, the windows of empty
    offices,
Empty schoolrooms, empty churches. O so much emptiness!
There is this cessation. This terrible cessation of everything.
These bodies mounded around me now, these polar sleepers—
What blue, moony ray ices their dreams?

I feel it enter me, cold, alien, like an instrument.
And that mad, hard face at the end of it, that O-mouth
Open in its gape of perpetual grieving.
It is she that drags the blood-black sea around
Month after month, with its voices of failure.
I am helpless as the sea at the end of her string.
I am restless. Restless and useless. I, too, create corpses.

I shall move north. I shall move into a long blackness.
I see myself as a shadow, neither man nor woman,
Neither a woman, happy to be like a man, nor a man
Blunt and flat enough to feel no lack. I feel a lack.
I hold my fingers up, ten white pickets.
See, the darkness is leaking from the cracks.
I cannot contain it. I cannot contain my life.

I shall be a heroine of the peripheral.
I shall not be accused by isolate buttons,

Holes in the heels of socks, the white mute faces
Of unanswered letters, coffined in a letter case.
I shall not be accused, I shall not be accused.
The clock shall not find me wanting, nor these stars
That rivet in place abyss after abyss.

THIRD VOICE:
I see her in my sleep, my red, terrible girl.
She is crying through the glass that separates us.
She is crying, and she is furious.
Her cries are hooks that catch and grate like cats.
It is by these hooks she climbs to my notice.
She is crying at the dark, or at the stars
That at such a distance from us shine and whirl.

I think her little head is carved in wood,
A red, hard wood, eyes shut and mouth wide open.
And from the open mouth issue sharp cries
Scratching at my sleep like arrows,
Scratching at my sleep, and entering my side.
My daughter has no teeth. Her mouth is wide.
It utters such dark sounds it cannot be good.

FIRST VOICE:
What is it that flings these innocent souls at us?
Look, they are so exhausted, they are all flat out
In their canvas-sided cots, names tied to their wrists,
The little silver trophies they've come so far for.
There are some with thick black hair, there are some bald.
Their skin tints are pink or sallow, brown or red;
They are beginning to remember their differences.

I think they are made of water; they have no expression.
Their features are sleeping, like light on quiet water.
They are the real monks and nuns in their identical garments.
I see them showering like stars on to the world—

47

On India, Africa, America, these miraculous ones,
These pure, small images. They smell of milk.
Their footsoles are untouched. They are walkers of air.

Can nothingness be so prodigal?
Here is my son.
His wide eye is that general, flat blue.
He is turning to me like a little, blind, bright plant.
One cry. It is the hook I hang on.
And I am a river of milk.
I am a warm hill.

SECOND VOICE:
I am not ugly. I am even beautiful.
The mirror gives back a woman without deformity.
The nurses give back my clothes, and an identity.
It is usual, they say, for such a thing to happen.
It is usual in my life, and the lives of others.
I am one in five, something like that. I am not hopeless.
I am beautiful as a statistic. Here is my lipstick.

I draw on the old mouth.
The red mouth I put by with my identity
A day ago, two days, three days ago. It was a Friday.
I do not even need a holiday; I can go to work today.
I can love my husband, who will understand.
Who will love me through the blur of my deformity
As if I had lost an eye, a leg, a tongue.

And so I stand, a little sightless. So I walk
Away on wheels, instead of legs, they serve as well.
And learn to speak with fingers, not a tongue.
The body is resourceful.
The body of a starfish can grow back its arms
And newts are prodigal in legs. And may I be
As prodigal in what lacks me.

48

She is a small island, asleep and peaceful,
And I am a white ship hooting: Goodbye, goodbye.
The day is blazing. It is very mournful.
The flowers in this room are red and tropical.
They have lived behind glass all their lives, they have been
    cared for tenderly.
Now they face a winter of white sheets, white faces.
There is very little to go into my suitcase.

There are the clothes of a fat woman I do not know.
There is my comb and brush. There is an emptiness.
I am so vulnerable suddenly.
I am a wound walking out of hospital.
I am a wound that they are letting go.
I leave my health behind. I leave someone
Who would adhere to me: I undo her fingers like bandages: I
    go.

SECOND VOICE:
I am myself again. There are no loose ends.
I am bled white as wax, I have no attachments.
I am flat and virginal, which means nothing has happened,
Nothing that cannot be erased, ripped up and scrapped, begun
    again.
These little black twigs do not think to bud,
Nor do these dry, dry gutters dream of rain.
This woman who meets me in windows—she is neat.

So neat she is transparent, like a spirit.
How shyly she superimposes her neat self
On the inferno of African oranges, the heel-hung pigs.
She is deferring to reality.
It is I. It is I—
Tasting the bitterness between my teeth.
The incalculable malice of the everyday.

FIRST VOICE:

How long can I be a wall, keeping the wind off?
How long can I be
Gentling the sun with the shade of my hand,
Intercepting the blue bolts of a cold moon?
The voices of loneliness, the voices of sorrow
Lap at my back ineluctably.
How shall it soften them, this little lullaby?

How long can I be a wall around my green property?
How long can my hands
Be a bandage to his hurt, and my words
Bright birds in the sky, consoling, consoling?
It is a terrible thing
To be so open: it is as if my heart
Put on a face and walked into the world.

THIRD VOICE:

Today the colleges are drunk with spring.
My black gown is a little funeral:
It shows I am serious.
The books I carry wedge into my side.
I had an old wound once, but it is healing.
I had a dream of an island, red with cries.
It was a dream, and did not mean a thing.

FIRST VOICE:

Dawn flowers in the great elm outside the house.
The swifts are back. They are shrieking like paper rockets.
I hear the sound of the hours
Widen and die in the hedgerows. I hear the moo of cows.
The colours replenish themselves, and the wet
Thatch smokes in the sun.
The narcissi open white faces in the orchard.

I am reassured. I am reassured.
These are the clear bright colours of the nursery,
The talking ducks, the happy lambs.
I am simple again. I believe in miracles.
I do not believe in those terrible children
Who injure my sleep with their white eyes, their fingerless
    hands.
They are not mine. They do not belong to me.

I shall meditate upon normality.
I shall meditate upon my little son.
He does not walk. He does not speak a word.
He is still swaddled in white bands.
But he is pink and perfect. He smiles so frequently.
I have papered his room with big roses,
I have painted little hearts on everything.

I do not will him to be exceptional.
It is the exception that interests the devil.
It is the exception that climbs the sorrowful hill
Or sits in the desert and hurts his mother's heart.
I will him to be common,
To love me as I love him,
And to marry what he wants and where he will.

THIRD VOICE:
Hot noon in the meadows. The buttercups
Swelter and melt, and the lovers
Pass by, pass by.
They are black and flat as shadows.
It is so beautiful to have no attachments!
I am solitary as grass. What is it I miss?
Shall I ever find it, whatever it is?

The swans are gone. Still the river
Remembers how white they were.

It strives after them with its lights.
It finds their shapes in a cloud.
What is that bird that cries
With such sorrow in its voice?
I am young as ever, it says. What is it I miss?

SECOND VOICE:
I am at home in the lamplight. The evenings are lengthening.
I am mending a silk slip: my husband is reading.
How beautifully the light includes these things.
There is a kind of smoke in the spring air,
A smoke that takes the parks, the little statues
With pinkness, as if a tenderness awoke,
A tenderness that did not tire, something healing.

I wait and ache. I think I have been healing.
There is a great deal else to do. My hands
Can stitch lace neatly on to this material. My husband
Can turn and turn the pages of a book.
And so we are at home together, after hours.
It is only time that weighs upon our hands.
It is only time, and that is not material.

The streets may turn to paper suddenly, but I recover
From the long fall, and find myself in bed,
Safe on the mattress, hands braced, as for a fall.
I find myself again. I am no shadow
Though there is a shadow starting from my feet. I am a wife.
The city waits and aches. The little grasses
Crack through stone, and they are green with life.

ACKNOWLEDGEMENTS

The poems have appeared in the *Observer*, the *New Statesman*, the *Review*, *Encounter*, *London Magazine*, the *New Yorker* and in *The New Poetry* (Penguin) edited by A. Alvarez, and *The Art of Sylvia Plath* (Faber and Faber), edited by C. Newman. 'Lesbos', 'The Swarm' and 'Mary's Song' were in the U.S. edition of *Ariel* published in 1966 by Harper & Row. A few of the poems appeared in *Crystal Gazer* and *Lyonnesse,* two collections of Sylvia Plath's poems, published in 1971 (Rainbow Press, London).

'Three Women' was first performed on the B.B.C. Third Programme, produced by Douglas Cleverdon, on 19th August, 1962. Cast: The Wife (First Voice): Penelope Lee; the Secretary (Second Voice): Jill Balcon; the Girl (Third Voice): Janette Richer. It was again produced by the B.B.C. Third Programme on 9th June, 1968. The Turret Books published 'Three Women', with an introduction by Douglas Cleverdon, in a limited edition of 180 copies in the winter of 1968. Excerpts have appeared in *Transatlantic,* the *Critical Quarterly*, the *Scotsman* and the *Quarterly Review of Literature.*